# Dementia and Estate Planning:
## Planning your estate after a diagnosis of Dementia

*Seven Truths about Dementia*

Douglas E. Koenig

Copyright © 2017 Douglas E. Koenig
Law Offices of Douglas E. Koenig, PLLC
2530 Meridian Parkway, Suite 300, Durham, NC 27713

All rights reserved.
ISBN: 1981856110
ISBN-13: 978-1981856114

The Publisher and Author make no representations or warranties with respect to the accuracy or completeness of the contents of this work and specifically disclaim all warranties, including without limitation warranties of fitness for a particular purpose. No warranty may be created or extended by sales or promotional materials.

The advice and strategies contained herein may not be suitable for every situation. This work is sold with the understanding that the publisher is not engaged in rendering legal, account or other professional services. If professional assistance is required, the services of a competent professional person should be sought. Neither the Publisher nor the Author shall be liable for damages arising here from use of any information in this book.

The fact that an organization or website is referred to in this work as a citation and/ or potential source of further information does not mean the that Author or Publisher endorses the information the organization or website may provide or recommendations it may make. Further, readers should be aware that the internet websites listed in this work may have changed or disappeared between when this work was written and when it was read.

# DEDICATION

Friends and family.

# CONTENTS

DEDICATION ............................................................... iii
CONTENTS .................................................................. v
ACKNOWLEDGMENTS ................................................. i
Why this book? ........................................................... 3
7 Truths About a Dementia Diagnosis and Estate Planning ........ 9
1. It can be a shock ................................................... 10
2. Dementia is many different things, not just Alzheimer's disease. ................................................................. 11
3. People accept the diagnosis differently ................. 16
4. Knowledge is power. ............................................. 18
5. Treatments differ for different dementias ............. 20
6. The patient AND the Caregiver both have to stay healthy .... 22
7. You need to handle legal matters as soon as possible. ......... 26
About the Author ....................................................... 32
Take Action Today! .................................................... 35

# ACKNOWLEDGMENTS

Reviewers

Cheryl

Friends

Alzheimer's Association

# WHY THIS BOOK?

We are all getting older.

Some of us **like** that thought ... it means being able to vote for the first time, or to go off to college. Or to serve our country in the military.

Getting older might mean the entry to new and exciting things.

For others of us, getting older is a scary thought. It brings images to mind that we simply would prefer to avoid. Sickness or hospitals, being cared for, having others make decisions about where we live and what we can do.

**Aging forces us to confront our own mortality.**

It is uncomfortable.
We stick our heads in the sand.

> *Aging forces us to confront our own mortality.*

How do I know this?

Law Offices of Douglas E. Koenig, PLLC
919-724-4778

My name is Doug Koenig, and I help people age with their dignity intact. I'm an attorney in Durham, North Carolina, with a law practice that focuses on the needs of elders and their families.

We provide peace of mind. We help people plan for getting older. We can help you too!

**I'm not just another attorney.**

Growing up in a military household, we were accustomed to the lifestyle of a serviceman. Dad was a Naval Aviator, and we spent time in some of the bases along the Gulf Coast.

I appreciate their sacrifices and I respect the men and women and families that make up our military.

Educated at Dartmouth, and then as an engineer at the Thayer School of Engineering, I know about sweating the details and planning too.

You can't build anything, much less a fighter plane or a bridge, without planning and thinking about the moving parts.

Later in my career I moved into computers and

the IT world. I worked with Digital Equipment, and then Ford Motor Company. Some of the work was international, so I learned how cultures and beliefs can affect planning.

Managing parts of many projects, large and small, I learned how to plan and to prepare for changes and detours and the unknown.

A key truth I learned is that you can prepare reasonably well for what you see coming ... the harder part is preparing for what you don't anticipate.

> *Planning is preparing*
> *for what you don't*
> *anticipate.*

**Did it apply to me? Yes, it did!**

Over time, I noticed that was no longer the young one in the crowd, and that I wasn't really wanting to work at a high-pressure job like I had when I really was younger. But, I didn't plan for change.

In 2006 I had the opportunity to retire from a

job and company I loved. But, it was a surprise because I had not planned.

All the decisions we made as part of that event were based on prayer and thoughtful consideration, and on good solid plans.

Following retirement, I wanted to help other people. After all, I now had the time!

Many options presented themselves, including church, volunteering, and, surprisingly, Law School. Investing in my own future through education was part of the plan and proved the best alternative.

After opening my own practice and working in general law, my mother faced surgeries and my wife's mother began to show signs of aging too. These changes called me into the field of "Elder Law" which is an area of practice dedicated to the needs to our elders and their families.

**We work with families.**

It begins, in our practice, with a family meeting as we begin to understand you and your family.

We like to know who you are, and what goals and wishes and dreams you have. No, this is not typical for an attorney, but then, you already know that I'm not your typical attorney.

Once we have the big-picture, we can look into the details. Whether it is planning for estates, or charitable giving, or retirement, or your health, we have tools and knowledge that can help you.

*Elder Law usually involves planning. A lot of it!*

**Why can I help you?**

First, I know what I'm talking about.

Everything I talk about is a real event or story I gleaned from my clients or my own experiences as a Navy brat or a civilian that helps me relate to your stories.

Second, I want to help you.

I didn't stay retired. I opened a practice aimed at elders and their needs. My staff and I want you to age gracefully and with dignity. We can help you with that.

Third, I'm right there with you.

Thinking about your own retirement? Worried about your aging parents? Concerned about your troubled children? I am too. I get it. I can help you.

I wrote this book as part of a series about common issues in Elder Law.

Read on, let's get started learning about "Planning for your Estate after a diagnosis of Dementia."

# 7 TRUTHS ABOUT A DEMENTIA DIAGNOSIS AND ESTATE PLANNING

**You do not need to fear a diagnosis. Read this book to learn more about dementia and what your next steps should be!**

Americans are living longer than ever, and as we age, more and more of us are hearing about illnesses that scare the bejeebers out of us! One of the most frightening is a diagnosis of dementia. And, it doesn't have to be "me" ... it could be a loved one, a neighbor, a trusted church friend.

It isn't a death sentence, but it might mean lifestyle changes. You can react many ways (and people do), but information, care and attention, and love for the one diagnosed will go a long way to making the years go by smoothly.

Here are seven truths about the diagnosis...

And ... important steps you should take NOW!

# 1. IT CAN BE A SHOCK

Receiving a diagnosis of dementia can be a difficult and emotional time. The diagnosis may come as a complete shock or it might provide answers to the problems you, or someone close to you, have been having. It can be hard to come to terms with it and know what to do next.

However, some people might even feel a sense of relief from knowing what is wrong and what steps to take. Some people who have been denying their issues to themselves and others may be forced to grapple with their situation. That isn't comfortable.

A loved one's diagnosis of Alzheimer's disease might be the most devastating and heartbreaking news you may ever have to face. Each day will bring on new challenges. But, you, and your loved ones, can get through it.

So, what is "dementia" anyway?

## 2. DEMENTIA IS MANY DIFFERENT THINGS, NOT JUST ALZHEIMER'S DISEASE.

The word dementia describes a set of <u>symptoms</u> that may include memory loss and problems with thinking, problem-solving or language. These changes are often small to start with, but for someone with a dementia diagnosis, the changes probably have become severe enough to affect daily life.

A person with dementia may also experience changes in their mood or behavior; some of these changes can vary by the day or even time-of-day.

The most common types of dementia include:
- <u>Alzheimer's disease</u> - This is the most common diagnosis of dementia. Problems with day-to-day memory are often noticed first, but other symptoms may include difficulties with: finding the right words, solving problems, making decisions, or perceiving things in three dimensions. Some researchers have noted that sense of smell can be an early indicator.
- <u>Vascular dementia</u> - If the oxygen supply to the brain is reduced because of narrowing

or blockage of blood vessels, some brain cells become damaged or die. The symptoms can occur either suddenly following one large stroke, or over time through a series of small strokes. Many people have difficulties with problem-solving or planning, thinking quickly and concentrating. Some of these effects are similar to symptoms from severe migraines. It is common for someone to have Alzheimer's disease and vascular dementia together.

- <u>Dementia with Lewy bodies</u> - This type of dementia involves tiny abnormal structures (Lewy bodies) developing inside brain cells. Early symptoms can include fluctuating alertness, difficulties with judging distances and hallucinations. Dementia with Lewy bodies is closely related to Parkinson's disease and often has some of the same symptoms, including difficulty with movement.
- <u>Frontotemporal dementia</u> (including Pick's disease) - In frontotemporal dementia, the front and side parts of the brain are damaged when clumps of abnormal proteins form inside nerve cells. At first, changes in personality and behavior may be

the most obvious signs. Depending on where the damage is, the person may have difficulties with fluent speech or may forget the meaning of words or objects.

Everyone experiences dementia differently.

Different types of dementia affect people differently, especially in the early stages. The specific symptoms that someone with dementia experiences will depend on the parts of the brain that are damaged and which disease is causing the dementia.

For someone who has been diagnosed, knowing the type of dementia they have can help them to understand some of the difficulties they may face, and ways to manage them.

Symptoms may differ with various kinds of dementia. For example, some dementias create "aphasia" which is the inability to choose and speak the correct words. For some, gait or stability might be affected. Or behavior and mood, or even sleep patterns. Some have delusions.

Often, early warnings are changes in "cognitive thinking". Here are some kinds of cognitive issues:

- <u>day-to-day or short-term memory</u> - difficulty recalling events that happened recently, or inability to create new memories
- <u>concentrating, planning or organizing</u> - difficulties making decisions, solving problems or carrying out a sequence of tasks (e.g., cooking a meal)
- <u>language</u> - difficulties following a conversation or finding the right word for something (aphasia)
- <u>visuospatial skills</u> - problems judging distances and seeing objects in three dimensions (this may be a particularly serious issue on stairs or outdoors)
- <u>orientation</u> - losing track of the day or date, or becoming confused about where they are

Occasionally, patients receive a diagnosis of "mild cognitive impairment". What does that mean?

This is a diagnosis when people have problems with their memory or thinking but not severe enough to interfere with everyday life. In this case, a doctor may diagnose mild cognitive impairment (MCI).

Research shows that people with MCI have an increased risk of developing dementia; about 10-15 per cent of this group will develop dementia each year.

However, MCI can also be caused by other conditions such as anxiety, depression, physical illness, substance abuse, and side effects of medication. Because of this, some people with MCI do not go on to develop dementia, and a small number of people will even get better.

There isn't a single test for dementia. It is diagnosed by a series of observations, usually at a memory clinic or neurosurgeon's office.

Sometimes the diagnosis is wrong initially, because some of the symptoms overlap.

The real cause probably isn't as critical as how you respond to it.

| Which leads us to the next truth... |
|---|

## 3. PEOPLE ACCEPT THE DIAGNOSIS DIFFERENTLY

Coming to terms with a diagnosis may take a long time and it may be gut-wrenching.

The person might experience a range of emotions, including shock, anger, fear, or even relief at having their symptoms explained. This is normal, and feelings may change from one day to the next. The person's friends and family are also likely to experience a range of emotions and their own difficulties coming to terms with what is happening.

It can help people to talk about their diagnosis, and how they feel about it, with family and friends.

Talking about things openly and honestly can help them to think about how they can support each other, and look at ways for the person to carry on living an independent and active life. Talking can also help the person think about the future.

The person may want to talk about their diagnosis with others as well. This could be a counsellor, a health or social care professional, or other people with dementia.

In some areas, including in the Duke Hospital system, there will be post-diagnosis support groups. This will help the person, and those close to them, come to terms with the diagnosis and look at ways to live well with dementia.

Who to tell about a diagnosis, and how much to say and when, are all up to the individual. They may be worried about how others might react. Whatever the person decides to do, it should be what they feel is right for them.

For some, it is very hard to accept the diagnosis.

Allow yourself time to let reality sink in.

Whether this diagnosis comes as a surprise or more of a confirmed suspicion, absorbing the changes ahead is a critical process. It is tremendously important to give yourself time to adjust to the magnitude of this disease.

| What can you do to begin to adjust? |
|---|

## 4. KNOWLEDGE IS POWER.

Although it may be very difficult at first, learning as much as you can about the disease will help you get through this process. You may find yourself overwhelmed with questions. How will our lives change? How long is life expectancy after diagnosis? How can I keep my loved one comfortable? The good news is that there are many resources to help you grasp what exactly you're dealing with. You are not alone. Seek help and encouragement.

Getting to know the common stages of Alzheimer's disease, caregiving practices and available treatments are very important. In addition, this gives you the opportunity to learn of stimulating activities and common practices that can help your loved one stay active and comfortable.

As with most confusing and scary things, being informed as quickly as possible is critical. The knowledge brings a sense of security and power in the face of an otherwise powerless feeling when the diagnosis is received.

## Ok, but, is there a pill I can take to make it better?

## 5. TREATMENTS DIFFER FOR DIFFERENT DEMENTIAS

As of yet, there is no cure for dementia. But, many new treatments can help slow the process down or treat important symptoms that are related to the dementia.

For someone with <u>vascular dementia</u>, the doctor might offer drugs that treat the underlying conditions (e.g., high blood pressure). These may help to slow the progression of dementia, although it won't generally reverse the effects.

A patient who has <u>dementia with Lewy bodies</u> might find that the doctor prescribes acetylcholinesterase inhibitors to help prevent symptoms such as hallucinations or delusions.

Someone with <u>frontotemporal dementia</u> may be prescribed an antidepressant.

Someone with mild to moderate <u>Alzheimer's disease</u> may be prescribed Aricept or a similar medication. These are called acetylcholinesterase inhibitors. As noted above, these drugs do not cure Alzheimer's, but may relieve memory problems and improve alertness for a while. Memantine is also given for severe dementia.

Of course, whether drugs help or not, there are many natural tools to use to reduce the effects of the disease or to adjust the tempo and rhythm of life.

For example, counseling, cognitive behavioral therapy, cognitive rehabilitation, and cognitive stimulation (including music) can be useful tools.

Working on memory skills, adding to your creative areas of life (such as music, art, or physical activity), and even other more exotic therapies can be used.

Each person may need to find the right combination of tools and tasks that help the best. And, it might differ from day to day ... so stay flexible and encouraging.

| So, Health is important, isn't it? |
| --- |

## 6. THE PATIENT AND THE CAREGIVER BOTH HAVE TO STAY HEALTHY

As the person suffering from progressive dementia, it is sometimes easy to fear the worst and act as if the end has come. But, try to stay independent as long as possible.

You will enjoy life longer when you enjoy life and not try to avoid it.

Having dementia does make everyday life more difficult, and a person with the condition (and their families) may need to change how they do things.

There are many new assistive technologies and gadgets that can help. These could include memory aids (e.g., clocks, calendars, and medication prompts, watches, and tablet software, and more) and electronics (e.g., falls sensors, GPS for those who might wander, motion and weight sensors, and so on). The list of support tools grows every day.

Dementia and Estate Planning

It is important that the person is shown how to use these aids properly, so they can get the best out of them. Assistive technology can also help people remain safer in their homes.

It is also very important to teach and learn as soon as possible. The sad fact is that dementia is usually progressive, so learning will become more of a challenge as time goes on. Learn how to use the new technology sooner rather than later!

It can help to think about changes that can be made in the home environment to enhance independence and safety. For example, it can be helpful to increase light levels and remove trip hazards such as loose rugs.

Your local care managers can be very helpful in designing your environment. Many of them will do home assessments, and may have connections with home renovation specialists.

In addition, the person with dementia might have difficulty articulating their needs. It may make them confused or forgetful, and unable to recall exactly when a new pain or symptom started.

Medication can cause side effects such as dizziness or increased confusion. Taking too many medications is risky, so you should always work with one pharmacist or doctor who knows all your meds, and bring the medication list along with you whenever you go to a specialist.

More things to consider ... regular checkups are essential. Don't forget about eyes, hearing, and diet. Some studies show that hearing is a significant risk factor in falls and awareness. So, check your hearing and be sure to have a supply of batteries available.

Finally, exercise. It has been shown that people who exercise have different body and brain chemistry, and that might affect much of life. Find exercises that people enjoy and that the patient and the caregiver can do together.

For the caregivers ... don't neglect *your* needs.

It is critical for caregivers to understand that taking care of yourself is an important aspect of caregiving. There are many roles you may have to take on as an Alzheimer's caregiver: cook, maid, accountant, chauffeur, and even nurse.

As the disease progresses, your loved one may not recognize you, remember what year it is, or know where they are. This perpetual stress wears on the caregiver.

Your mental and physical well-being is important for the cause, and there are many warning signs of caregiver stress.

Difficulty sleeping, staying focused or chronic headaches or mood swings (sounds like the person suffering from dementia, doesn't it?) can all be attributed to the stresses involved with caregiving.

Take a few minutes each day for yourself to do something you enjoy. Talk to friends and family members about your journey in caregiving. Join a support group. Exercise. Stay active.

> What else should I worry about, down the road?

## 7. YOU NEED TO HANDLE LEGAL MATTERS AS SOON AS POSSIBLE.

Someone who has received a diagnosis of dementia may want to spend some time thinking about the future and their wishes. An early diagnosis is not a limitation on your capacity.

Many of our elder clients have Alzheimer's, and are perfectly capable of making decisions. But, it is a progressive disease, and sadly, your capacity for making decisions will decline.

As the condition progresses, it will become more difficult for them to make decisions about their health, care (including end-of-life care) and finances. It is essential that you make decisions and finalize documents while you can.

Of course, a diagnosis does not mean that you lack capacity. But, it does mean that you might have a limited amount of time to get everything done. So, find a resource to help, such as an Elder Law attorney who understands the needs of persons with dementia and knows how to assess their capacity and plans.

# Dementia and Estate Planning

Life and planning for eventualities is a process; whatever diagnosis or illness you have, planning is essential. And, capacity varies from day-to-day, so, it is always a good idea to plan. You never really know exactly when you will need the plan.

The first documents to get in place are the various powers of attorney. If you do not have a valid Power of Attorney, your agent will not be legally able to make decisions (within the scope of the granted powers).

In the most general sense, to be fully protected, you will need the following:
- Financial Power of Attorney;
- Health care Power of Attorney,
- An Advance directive for health care, and
- Release of private health information.

You should do these documents while you are competent to make decisions. If you wait too long, no one will be able to help you sign this document.

You might also want to ask for help in such areas as running a business or making investment decisions. It is also important to have a Power of attorney when one spouse owns assets in their name alone.

What if you don't have a power of attorney?

If the person with dementia has a need for a decision, but no one has a valid power granted to them as agent, and a decision <u>must</u> be made, then a guardianship might be required. They are not used for one decision, of course, but as a last resort. Guardianships are expensive processes and begin with a petition filed at the Clerk of Superior Court.

There are many other tools for planning. For example:

- <u>A Last Will and Testament</u> tells people your wishes after your death. This is a specialized document that will be too late to help you while you are living. Wills can be used to direct your assets into trusts (which have their own rules), or to give ("devise") real property (houses or land) to others.

- <u>Trusts</u> (*Living, Irrevocable, or Special Needs*) can support incapacity planning as well, and the "Trustee" (the person assigned to manage the Trust assets) performs in a similar role as the Agent. A Trust serves a similar purpose to Powers of Attorney because it lets the trustee make decisions with the assets in the Trust. In some cases, you can be the trustee of your own Trust. Trusts absolutely require the help of an attorney.

- <u>Owning assets jointly</u> is another way to control decisions ... Joint Ownership of assets (*a high risk*) can include different kinds of ownership, including Joint Tenancy with Right of Survivorship, Tenants in Common, or Tenancy by the Entireties. Bank accounts or investment accounts can be owned in some of these ways, and some bank accounts can have a Pay-on-death ("POD") provision.

In a very broad sense, even Gifts can be a form of decision-making delegation, although you probably will *lose control of assets*.

You might be asking why you need an attorney for these decisions.

Elder Law attorneys think about different topics and issues than a general practitioner or an on-line form might (not that an on-line form actually "thinks").

For example, we elder law attorneys often consider what happen during a period of *incapacity*.

Most legal documents or processes assume you have some degree of capacity to *understand* ... such as the "intent" to commit a crime, or the ability to understand right from wrong. But, in the elder law world, many of our clients or their parents face a time of growing fear of "incapacity," or temporary or permanent loss of the decision-making powers.

We help the family address this issue, including both the powers to be shared and the agents to be chosen. We even offer training for agents so they understand their important roles. Each client, each family is different. Your plan has to fit your needs.

If you worry about your diagnosis, or that of a loved one, a very important course of action is to consult an attorney.

> **You may contact us for a free consultation by calling**
> **919-883-2800**

Don't wait too long.

Plan before you need to execute the plan.

=== The Law Offices of ===
# DOUGLAS E. KOENIG
=== *PLLC* ===

# ABOUT THE AUTHOR

Attorney Douglas E. Koenig

- Estate Planning
- Medicaid Planning
- Incapacity Planning
- Special Needs Trusts
- Veteran's Benefits
  (A&A and SCD)

I'm a Navy brat, said in the kindest of terms! As a child in a military family, I understand the unique challenges of military life from that perspective. Yes, moving all over the Gulf Coast, making new friends, and having dad deployed for long periods ... it is what we all went through together. And, as a result, I appreciate the sacrifice of those who have chosen to serve in the armed forces.

Most recently, I'm a graduate of the Michigan State University College of Law where I was involved in the business law and alternative dispute resolution programs. The College of Law is an established and accomplished institution in many areas and is a top 100 law school at a Big Ten University.

I completed undergraduate work at Dartmouth College and hold a degree in Materials Engineering from Thayer School of Engineering. My history and prior engineering and business experience contribute a strong foundation to my Juris Doctor, and my service to you!

In 2010, I established a compassionate Elder Law practice, which is focused on four main areas, including Veteran's benefits, Medicaid planning and crisis response, Special Needs Trusts, and Estate Planning and the related wills, trusts, and powers of attorney.

Not everyone can afford legal representation, so when appropriate, I offer time and expertise to various programs, including LEAP (via the NC Bar Association), Legal Aid of North Carolina, the UNC Pro Bono Cancer Clinic, and other organizations.

My other service time includes the Durham Downtown Rotary Club and the Gideons.

When we meet, be sure to ask about my work with Digital Equipment Corporation and Ford Motor Company in Michigan prior to locating in North Carolina. I have found connections with my clients through shared work experiences all over the world!

Church matters are important too and so I spend time participating in and leading bible study groups (in case you are invited, Bible Study Fellowship is a wonderful organization!).

I also enjoy sailing, photography, traveling, and, of course, friends and family! This year, my wife and I will have been married for 39 years, and we have three grown children and two grandchildren.

## TAKE ACTION TODAY!

Don't let dementia stop you from planning.
Take action today toward CLARITY ABOUT YOUR FUTURE!

*Call our office TODAY!
Make your appointment for a
FREE CONSULTATION
(A $500 value)*

# Take CONTROL Of Your Future and Your Legacy!

## Call: 919-724-4778

### The Law Offices of Douglas E. Koenig, PLLC

*www.dougkoeniglaw.com*

*Your Future Awaits!*

www.ingramcontent.com/pod-product-compliance
Lightning Source LLC
Chambersburg PA
CBHW031958240526
45464CB00024B/1310